DEMOCRACY

Xina M. Uhl and Bill Stites

rosen publishing's
rosen central

New York

Published in 2020 by The Rosen Publishing Group, Inc.
29 East 21st Street, New York, NY 10010

Copyright © 2020 by The Rosen Publishing Group, Inc.

First Edition

Library of Congress Cataloging-in-Publication Data

Names: Uhl, Xina M., author. | Stites, Bill, author.
Title: Democracy / Xina M. Uhl and Bill Stites.
Description: New York : Rosen Central, 2020. | Series: Examining political systems |
Audience: Grades 5–8. | Includes bibliographical references and index.
Identifiers: LCCN 2018019065| ISBN 9781508184515 (library bound) | ISBN 9781508184508 (pbk.)
Subjects: LCSH: Democracy—Juvenile literature.
Classification: LCC JC423 .U38 2019 | DDC 321.8—dc23
LC record available at https://lccn.loc.gov/2018019065

Manufactured in the United States of America

On the cover: Three symbols of democracy are the Statue of Liberty Enlightening the World, better known as simply the Statue of Liberty (*left*), a representation of the Constitution, the basis for the United States' government (*upper right*), and the first US president, George Washington (*lower right*).

CONTENTS

INTRODUCTION

Two contrasting forms of government rule the world today: democracies and autocracies. The power in autocratic governments resides in one person or group. A clear line exists between the leadership and the followers. The behavior of followers is highly controlled by the leadership, and followers have little say over their lives and circumstances. Citizens must not openly display disagreement with the government or defy the power of the leaders. A guarantee of civil liberties such as the ability to gather in groups or to voice opinions that may differ from the official ones does not exist.

In democracies, the power of government rests with the people. Decision-making power does not rest in one person or group. Instead, it is shared amongst others at different levels of authority, such as federal (nationwide), state or province (a region smaller than a nation), and local (a region smaller than a state or province such as a county or city). No clear line exists between those who run the government and those who do not. The government exerts less control over the lives and circumstances of the people. People are free to form political parties and participate in government. They can gather in large groups and they can speak out without fear of punishment, even if they voice opinions at odds with the rulers.

The majority of the world's modern governments are democracies today. In 1816, a little over nine million people lived under democratic rule. In 1915, this number was about 249 million. By 2015, more

Members of the Peloponnesian League came to Sparta in 432 BCE to air their grievances against another Greek city-state, Athens. The ancient Greeks took their responsibilities as citizens seriously.

than four billion of the world's estimated seven billion people lived under democracies. The consequences for the populations living under democracies are many. As opposed to populations living under autocracies, democracies are wealthier (except for a few countries that produce fossil fuels), healthier, better educated, and enjoy better protection of human rights.

From its beginning in Ancient Greece, democracy laid dormant for hundreds of years until just over two hundred years ago with the establishment of a democratic government in the

United States. At the beginning of the United States, true freedom was experienced by white male landowners. At the present time, people of all economic classes, racial groups, and both genders have the freedom to vote and participate in government. The meaning of democracy has evolved, and will likely continue to do so.

The basis of democracy is equality. In an an ideal democracy, everyone's opinion counts equally. In reality, this form of complete democracy has never been achieved. And it may never be. But this goal has, over the long centuries of human existence, been slowly tipping the balance toward freedom.

The pages that follow examine the foundations of democracy and those who influenced it most profoundly. The texts, correspondence, and ideas of such individuals are looked at, as is the world events and circumstances that caused changes and disruptions in forms of government. Democracy as a concept and as a reality has developed in response to abusive governments that have gone before it and that continue to exist in many parts of the world today.

CHAPTER 1

ANCIENT GOVERNMENTS

The Greek city-states that ruled in the rocky, mountainous terrain of both mainland and islands of the Aegean Sea saw the first development of democracy. The people engaged in

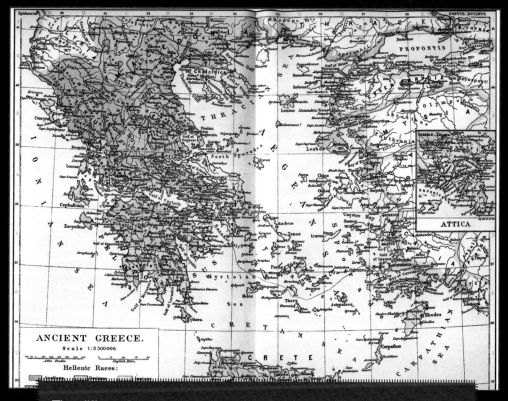

ANCIENT GREECE.

Scale 1:3 500 000.

Hellenic Races:

The differently-colored territories here represent the areas settled by various Greek peoples during ancient times. Modern Greek territory does not include land on the eastern shores of the Aegean Sea.

government with enthusiasm, and experimented with its forms in ways that influenced many rulers for centuries afterward.

Ancient Greece was not a single country. There were more than 1,500 distinct city-states sprawling across the land. Each had its own government, completely separate from its neighbors. And each of them had a different kind of government.

CITY-STATES AND GOVERNMENT

The Greek people had a passion for government. They enjoyed tinkering with it, trying new things, and seeing what worked and what didn't. The city-states borrowed ideas and methods from one another. The English word "politics" comes from the Ancient Greek *polis*, for city-state. Many of our other political words also come from Greek, including the word "democracy."

There were many different types of government at work in Greece. The ancient Greeks are famous for having developed democracy. But democracies were actually rare. Only two of the city-states gave democracy a serious try. And neither one lasted for long. In fact, the major Greek philosophers agreed that democracy was the worst form of government. Until very recently, most people in history would have agreed with them.

DEVELOPMENT OF DEMOCRACY

But the Greeks understood democracy very differently than any society since. "Democracy" is a combination of two Greek words, meaning "people" and "rule." The Greeks took it to mean exactly that—each citizen participated in the process of government. The form of democracy we practice today is called "representative democracy." That means we elect representatives to govern for us. Such ideas would have been alien to the Greeks. To them, democracy meant that every single citizen participated in running the city-state.

This did not mean that every person participated in government, though. Certain people could not become full citizens, such as women. Slavery was legal, and slaves couldn't be citizens. Neither could anyone who didn't own land. (Though, to be fair, that was also true in early America and other modern democracies.) Even a person whose family had been in a city-state for less than three generations could not be a citizen.

In most democracies today, every adult can vote. But very few people ever have a hand in running their government. In ancient

Called the "Bema" or "Vema" of Pnyx, popular assemblies took place on this stone platform in Athens, Greece. This assembly spot is a hill west of the Acropolis in use since the sixth century BCE.

Greece, very few people could vote, but those who did could play a direct role in their government.

The main governmental body in Athens was called the Assembly. That's where all the important decisions of running the city-state were made. The Assembly was huge: every single citizen of Athens was a member. That meant up to 45,000 people could vote on each proposed bill. The Athenians liked to involve as many people as possible in their government. Six thousand people had to be present before a meeting of the Assembly could even begin. Athenian juries typically had 501 people on them.

COUNCIL AND ASSEMBLY

The Athenians expected a lot of their citizens. The Assembly met forty times a year and every citizen had to attend regularly. But the Assembly couldn't handle all of the city-state's business because some people had to work full-time. Thus, there was a smaller group that met more often. It was called the Council of 500. It drafted the legislation that the Assembly voted on.

The 500 members of the council weren't elected as they would be today. They were selected randomly, by lot. Every citizen had an equal chance of being picked. There were also strict term limits. No one could serve on the council for more than two years. So more than 40 percent of Athens's citizens held office during their lives. That meant that more than 40 percent of the people in the Assembly had a firsthand understanding of how the government worked. The Athenians attempted to let every citizen help govern in as many ways as possible. They thought that the more involved a citizen was, the more wisely he would vote—and that would strengthen the democracy.

These clay juror tables, also known as ballot papers, date from the fifth century BCE. They were used in meetings of the board of the Eleven, public officials in Athens who were in charge of all executions.

The Athenians felt that the citizens of a city-state had to share the work of governing. If they didn't, the government would not serve everyone's interests. But they excluded women and other large groups of people from their government. And the Assembly never took those people's issues and interests seriously. By preventing them from participating in the democracy, the Athenians silenced their voices. The Greeks felt strongly that every citizen had to have equal voice in order for the democracy to be fair. But not every person's voice was equal. So corruption and injustice were a fact of life. The citizens were generally treated very well by the government. But the noncitizens were not. Our idea of democracy today is that it has to include everyone, or else it can never be fair.

EXECUTION OF SOCRATES

Another unusual aspect of the Greek democracies was that it never occurred to them that individuals should have rights. The way they saw it, the government was nothing more than the combined will of the citizens. So there was no reason why people would need civil rights to protect them from the

A SLAVE'S LIFE

Ancient Greek citizens spent much of their waking hours participating in government. They also spent time learning and debating philosophy with one another. They were able to engage in these pursuits because they did not have to work—they had slaves for that. People became slaves in one of several ways: they were born into it, kidnapped, captured in war by enemy soldiers, or captured by pirates and sold.

Slaves were considered private property. Under the law, slaves could be forced to work, beaten, sold, and sometimes even killed. Slaves were treated differently according to what jobs they performed and where they lived. Athenians were better to their slaves than other city-states. In Athens, the most respected slaves served as tutors or police officials. The next most respected were domestic servants that lived within the home and took care of daily tasks such as cooking and child-rearing. Some slaves became soldiers for their masters. Low status slaves worked in the fields and as manual laborers, and those of the lowest status worked in dangerous, deadly silver mines.

In Athens, slaves had some protection under the law. They also might be permitted to earn money of their own to purchase their freedom. Neither of these were the case in Sparta, where slaves, called helots, endured harsh treatment. In Sparta, slaves may have outnumbered citizens by twenty to one. Citizens lived in fear of slave revolts.

government. It was a nice idea. But it resulted in some terrible mistakes.

The great philosopher Socrates was sentenced to death for blasphemy by the Assembly. Socrates knew he'd been falsely accused. But he believed in democracy. So he chose to respect his countrymen's wishes and poison himself. But his student Plato never forgave the Assembly for his teacher's death. He always harbored a great distrust of democracy. Plato's works and those of his student Aristotle were widely read in Europe for thousands of years after that. They both opposed democracy. So they influenced a great many powerful Europeans into opposing it as well. By killing Socrates, the Athenians killed off democracy for a long time to come.

LEGACY OF ANCIENT DEMOCRACY

The fact that Socrates was an Athenian is powerful proof of the good democracy can do. The brief period in which democracy flourished in Ancient Greece left us with some of the greatest writing the world has ever seen. The playwrights and philosophers of Athens are still widely read today. During Athens's democratic period, the Parthenon was built. By letting an unparalleled part of the population participate in the work of governing themselves, the Athenians inspired their citizens in a way few cultures have since.

Unfortunately, democracy in Greece didn't last. Invading armies eventually conquered Athens. When they did, democracy ended. But Plato's and Aristotle's histories remained.

Those two men hated democracy. But their record of it inspired people anyway. Eventually, some Europeans began to wonder if the Greeks had been on to something. By then, Europe was firmly under the control of its kings and queens. There was no way for democracy to gain a foothold. A new continent would have to be conquered for democracy to have the blank slate it needed to begin anew.

CHAPTER 2

DEMOCRACY IS BORN AGAIN

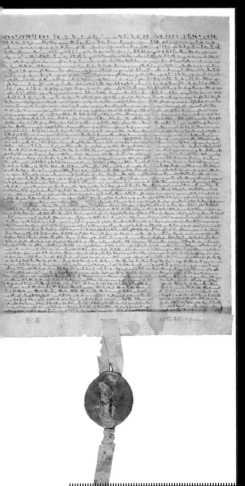

In 404 BCE, Sparta conquered Athens, and ended democracy there. Hundreds of years passed before democracy would regain a footing in the west. Small, but significant steps were made toward democracy when in England King John's nobles forced him to sign the Magna Carta in 1215. The English Parliament had also earned a degree of power that allowed them to put some limitations on the crown. Nevertheless, monarchy flourished throughout Europe.

GOVERNMENT BY MONARCHY

For centuries, royal families had promoted the theory of the divine

After agreeing to his barons' demands, King John authorized that handwritten copies of the Magna Carta be prepared and read throughout England. One of these copies is shown here. See page 50 for a partial transcription.

right of kings. They claimed they ruled through God's will. How else would they rule if they did not have God's help? The church helped royalty keep an iron grip on their power for a long time.

But in the early 1600s, their grip began to loosen. The growth of the middle class made it harder for monarchs to keep their subjects in line. The Catholic Church broke up into many factions, reducing its power. Philosophers such as John Locke, Jean-Jacques Rousseau, and Thomas Hobbes questioned the nature of government.

As this happened, people were settling in the colonies in America. Many of them were victims of religious persecution. They braved the long trip to America to find a place where they could worship freely. Unlike anyplace else, freedom and independence were always crucial parts of the American character.

At first, England, France, Holland, and other countries controlled parts of America's eastern coast. The only way colonists could communicate with their mother countries was by sending messages by ship. But it took a long time to receive an answer. So the colonists developed local governments to handle day-to-day matters. After a while, some of the colonists began to question why they should answer to a country across the ocean.

A DEMOCRATIC REVOLUTION

By the late 1700s, the situation between England and the colonies had gotten ugly. War between the government and its subjects became inevitable. This was not the first time such a thing had happened. But it would be the first time that the men behind a revolution would seek democracy as their remedy.

George Washington, Thomas Jefferson, and the other architects of the revolution were wealthy. If America had had a royal class, they certainly would have been part of it. They were also scholars. They had read Locke and Rousseau. They had studied the ancient Greeks. They had seen firsthand how religious freedom had benefited American society. And they began to think about extending that freedom in other ways.

THE CONTINENTAL CONGRESSES

In 1774, representatives from twelve of the thirteen colonies met in Philadelphia. They called the meeting the Continental Congress. Almost immediately, they issued a list of grievances they had with their king. By 1775, the king had not yet responded to their demands. So the Continental Congress met again. Now they would develop a plan to unify the colonies.

THE DECLARATION OF INDEPENDENCE

By July 1776, the colonists had lost all hope that they could resolve their problems with the British king. The time had come to formally separate from England. So the colonists sent delegates to a meeting in Philadelphia to write another statement. Thomas Jefferson was regarded as the best writer among them, so he was made the head of the committee. He was to be the primary author of the Declaration of Independence.

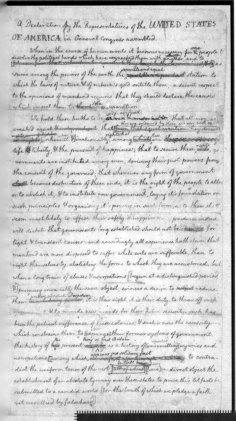

This is a page from Jefferson's original rough draft of the Declaration of Independence. John Adams and Benjamin Franklin made the revisions above the crossed out portions. See pages 50–51 for a partial transcription.

THE IROQUOIS CONFEDERATION

Scholars debate whether America's government was partially inspired by the political system of the Iroquois.

The Iroquois Confederation began in about 1450, and consisted of Five Nations that shared common languages and cultures: Oneida, Onondaga, Cayuga, Mohawk, and Seneca. In the eighteenth century, the Tuscarora joined the confederation and it became the Six Nations. The confederation passed their rules and laws down orally, and developed democracy even before they created written language. They called their constitution the Great Binding Law.

The Great Binding Law created a single governmental body for all the Iroquois called the Great Council. Each nation was equally represented. The women of each tribe selected the representatives to the Great Council.

In 1744, Canasatego lead the Onondaga nation, and spoke for the Iroquois Confederation. He told the British colonists:

. . . We heartily recommend Union and a Good Agreement between you our Brethren. Our wise Forefathers established Union and Amity between the Five Nations; this has made us formidable, this has given us great weight and Authority with our Neighboring Nations. We are a Powerfull confederacy, and by your observing the same Methods our wise Forefathers have taken, you will acquire fresh Strength and Power.

There is no doubt that framers of the US Constitution admired the Iroquois system, which established a system of checks and balances by

(continued on the next page)

(continued from the previous page)

which disputes among the tribes could be settled. While scholars continue to argue about whether the Iroquois confederation strongly influenced the forming of the Constitution, it remains a distinct possibility that it did.

IMMORTAL WORDS

Jefferson had been given a task no one before him had ever undertaken. Not only did he have to announce the birth of a democracy, but he also had to justify democracy to the world. He spent about two weeks drafting the declaration. The document he created was as revolutionary as any ever set to paper.

The second paragraph of the Declaration of Independence begins: "We hold these truths to be self-evident, that all men are created equal, that they are endowed by their Creator with certain unalienable Rights, that among these are Life, Liberty and the pursuit of Happiness." There is no precedent for what Jefferson did with these words. There was no country on Earth at the time in which people were guaranteed liberty. But Jefferson had the courage to stand up and announce that all humans shared certain rights, which no government could take away from them. He was even bold enough to say that this was so clear as to be "self-evident." That seems natural to most of us today, but at the time it shocked the world. He may have thought the things he said were obvious. But there were a lot of people at the time who disagreed with him.

The declaration is unique because it's not a political document. It is not a constitution. It is a statement of beliefs. Jefferson had no idea when he wrote it what form democracy in America would take. But he set a standard for what it should be, and the country

This circa 1776 engraving by Edward Savage is entitled *Congress Voting the Declaration of Independence*. In it, Thomas Jefferson lays the declaration on the table at right, while other members of the Constitutional Congress look on.

has been working toward that ever since. For the first time in history, a government would be founded on a noble principle. America was started as a place that would protect the rights of all its citizens. In one sentence, Jefferson shook the institution of monarchy to its core.

Jefferson went on to write the following in the Declaration of Independence: "That to secure these rights, Governments

Gilbert Stuart painted this portrait of Thomas Jefferson in 1805. When he was just thirty-three years old, Jefferson served as the principal author of the Declaration of Independence.

are instituted among Men, deriving their just powers from the consent of the governed." The phrase "consent of the governed" comes from John Locke. Those words were very dangerous to the people in power at the time. They represented a complete disregard of the theory of divine right. To Locke, the citizens wielded the real power. Their rulers could only rule them if they allowed themselves to be ruled. By implying that a people could take away their consent to be governed, his words inherently justify revolution.

And so Jefferson followed them by announcing one when he wrote, "That whenever any Form of Government becomes destructive of these ends, it is the Right of the People to alter or abolish it, and to institute new Government, laying its foundation on such principles and organizing its powers in such form, as to them shall seem most likely to effect their Safety and Prudence."

That sentence, like the one before it, overturns a centuries-old concept of government. Rather than a nation's citizens being completely subjugated to an absolute monarch appointed by

God, for the first time a people were announcing that government existed to serve them and was theirs to decide.

After listing the reasons why the colonies should rebel against the king, Jefferson finished with a phrase that justified many more democratic revolutions in the coming decades: "A Prince whose character is thus marked by every act which may define a Tyrant, is unfit to be the ruler of a free people." For the first time, a free people were overturning their majesty's right to rule them.

That Jefferson's words still hold so much power to this day is a testament to his wisdom. He must have known that it would be a long time before any government treated all men as though they were created equal. But he knew his words would live longer than he would. They would give the new country a purpose. They gave all Americans a goal.

JEFFERSON AND SLAVERY

Jefferson himself had a complicated relationship with freedom. He owned slaves and did not grant most of them freedom upon his death, as many of his fellow revolutionaries did. But he also tried to include a statement in the declaration condemning the slave trade. Unfortunately, men from the Southern states would not allow it.

Jefferson seemed to understand that slavery was an abomination, yet he could not bring himself to rebel against it the way he did against the king. But by including that groundbreaking phrase in the declaration — "all men are created equal" — he gave a powerful weapon to those fighting for freedom in the centuries ahead. He cast a beacon of light to the entire world. Eventually his words would help to free millions of people, including America's slaves.

CHAPTER 3

THE AMERICAN EXPERIMENT

Thomas Jefferson gave a powerful voice to democracy when he wrote the Declaration of Independence. The Second Continental Congress supported that voice on July 4, 1776 when they adopted the declaration. However, a formidable task remained. How would America make democracy work?

After the American Revolution, most Americans were scared to give the government too much power—the king had abused them for a long time. The Second Continental Congress had been inspired by Jefferson's eloquent declaration, and it wanted to see how well America could work with as little government as possible. So the delegates devised a system that gave the Congress just enough power to accomplish what they felt was really needed. All other rights and powers were reserved for the individual states. Congress coined a name for its new country that stuck: the United States of America.

A POWER STRUCTURE

The delegates could not agree on how the federal government should work. It took them years to resolve all their arguments. The small states thought every state's voice should count equally,

Gilbert Stuart's 1779 portrait of sixty-four-year-old George Washington shows him renouncing his third term as president. Washington died at age sixty-seven at his beloved estate, Mount Vernon, in Virginia.

because they didn't want to get overshadowed. The big states said that if every state had equal power, they should all pay equal taxes. Of course, the small states wouldn't agree to that. The debate about slavery very nearly brought the whole process to a halt.

THE ARTICLES OF CONFEDERATION

The agreement that Congress came up with for America's first federal government was called the Articles of Confederation. After much revision, eventually all of the states were willing to give it a shot. But by the time the articles were ratified, it was clear that they weren't going to work out.

Under the Articles of Confederation, the individual states were more like separate countries. Congress had very little power over them. In the absence of a strong federal government, several states had made their own treaties with other countries. Nine states had their own armies, and several had their own navies. Most of the states had their own currency, making exchange and trade between the states very difficult. Congress lacked the power to levy taxes. So it was always short of the money it needed for vital services. Within five years, the articles collapsed.

The first attempt to design a federal government failed. No one had ever attempted to establish a democracy on that scale before. The colonies were much bigger than the Greek city-states that had inspired them. No one had ever dealt with the problems they were facing. Delegates learned their lesson quickly, though. If the states were to be united, the federal government would have to be more powerful than they were. Each state would have to sacrifice some of its independence for the good of the whole.

On May 25, 1787, representatives from each colony met in Philadelphia to address the problems created by the Articles of Confederation. This meeting, which lasted for four grueling months, came to be known as the Constitutional Convention.

MARYLAND VS. VIRGINIA

A trade dispute between Maryland and Virginia spelled the end for the Articles of Confederation. Under the articles, Congress did not have the power to regulate trade between the states.

The states had rejected the oversight of Congress, but this left them without a means of settling disagreements between states, and without a way to enforce decisions about such disagreements. The only hope was to find a workable compromise, at the bargaining table. In September 1786, representatives from five states gathered in Maryland to try to settle the matter.

The discussion was long and tense. Finally, Alexander Hamilton, the delegate from New York, had the courage to stand up and say that the problem they faced was bigger than the matter at hand. If they managed to solve the Maryland and Virginia problem it did not matter. Other problems would arise

(continued on the next page)

The Articles of Confederation consisted of thirteen articles. Though it was approved by Congress in 1777, it was not ratified until 1781. See partial transcription on page 51.

(continued from the previous page)

soon enough. The Articles of Confederation did not provide an adequate system to solve such problems. They were not going to work long term.

Hamilton proposed that the issue be put aside and a meeting be scheduled for the next spring. In May 1787, representatives from all the states would come together to discuss the need for a stronger national government. The meeting, when it came, resulted in the formation of the US Constitution.

Once again, delegates turned to the philosophers for inspiration. They found their solution in the writings of the Baron de Montesquieu and John Locke. The secret was to divide the power so it wouldn't be invested in one place. Because Congress was the only federal body under the articles, the states had insisted that it be weak. To give one body so much control would be too much like a monarchy.

A CONVENTION MEETS

The matter of how to fairly represent all the states was a big stumbling block. The last time around, the debate had taken years. Now the Constitutional Convention was starting from scratch. Inevitably, the representation issue reared its head. It was clear that the federal government under the articles had been too weak. The new Congress was going to have the power to start wars, levy taxes, and negotiate treaties. So every state wanted to have as much power as it could. Thus, the whole debate began again.

Fortunately, this time the men at the convention found a solution quickly. They took a lesson from England's Parliament, which was

Thomas Jefferson drafted the Declaration of Independence in rooms he rented from bricklayer Jacob Graff. The National Park Service reconstructed the house in 1975. It is part of Independence National Historical Park in Philadelphia, Pennsylvania.

split into two separate houses. America's legislature would also have two different houses. Both of them would need to approve a bill before it could become a law. They called the larger house the House of Representatives. The smaller they called the Senate. Representation for the House would be determined by a state's population. In the Senate, all states would be represented equally. That way, both the small and the large states would be happy.

THREE BRANCHES OF GOVERNMENT

The men at the convention devised a system that gave equal power to each of three separate branches of government. While individual states would have to sacrifice some of their freedom to federal power, none of the three branches of government could wield that power with impunity.

This was called a system of checks and balances. If any branch of the government overstepped its boundaries, the other two would be there to keep it in check. They could balance its power with their own. The first branch would be legislative, made up of representatives from every state, which would make laws. The second would be the executive, headed by a president, who would enforce the laws. The last would be the judicial, whose job it was to interpret the laws.

THE PROBLEM OF SLAVERY

But there was one more huge issue facing the convention: slavery. The slave states wanted their slave populations to count toward their representation. That way, they'd have more power in the new Congress. But they didn't want their slaves to count toward their taxation. The nonslave states felt it should be the other way around.

If this were the first time America had gone down this road, the debate might have gone on for a very long time. It certainly would have gotten ugly. However, all of the delegates had a few things in common. They knew America needed a stronger federal government. They also knew that they couldn't spend as long arguing as they did when writing the Articles of Confederation. The problems would have to be solved soon, or democracy in America would fail.

Before long, the delegates reached a compromise. Slaves would be counted, for representation and taxation, but at only three-fifths of their true number. The Northern states were willing to agree to that because it meant more taxes for the treasury, which they wouldn't have to pay. But it didn't give the Southern states too much power in Congress. For the Southern states, the extra taxes seemed worth the extra voice in Congress.

There were some in the convention, including Benjamin Franklin, who passionately opposed slavery. But they knew that any attempt to outlaw or regulate slavery would alienate the Southern states. The Union was so young that it could not afford to create such a rift yet. So even the antislavery delegates agreed to the three-fifths compromise and left it at that. They knew full well that the slavery question would have to be settled in some way later. But for the time being, they thought it was more important to keep

THE UNITED STATES CONSTITUTION

Between the checks and balances principle and the three-fifths compromise, most of the concerns about a stronger national government had been allayed. By September 1787, the convention was able to come up with a draft of the new Constitution that was

Every clause of the United States Constitution of 1787 came from the Articles of Confederation, the Northwest Ordinance, or state constitutions. See page 52 for a partial transcription.

acceptable to everyone present. The states were by then so eager to move beyond the mess the Articles of Confederation had created that most of them put aside any problems they might have with the new Constitution.

By June of the next year, the Constitution had been ratified, and the most complex system of government ever devised was set into motion. Except for the horrors of the Civil War, the system embodied by the Constitution has been successful enough to keep the Union not only intact but growing ever since.

CHANGE THROUGH AMENDMENTS

The framers' final bit of genius was to set out a clear system through which the Constitution could be changed. The delegates at the Constitutional Convention had a crucial bit of foresight. They knew that, no matter what, no system could be perfect. As history unfolded, someday it would need to be changed. They made it difficult, but possible, for the Constitution to change with the times. Since its creation, constitutional amendments have extended the right to vote to blacks, women, and eighteen-to twenty-year-olds. The Supreme Court has repeatedly reinterpreted the meaning of some of the Constitution's key passages, extending rights to groups that had previously been denied them. Even the Bill of Rights, the source of some of our most cherished rights as Americans, was not originally a part of the Constitution.

The framers of the constitution gave democracy in America the room to grow and mature beyond their limited view. Had they not, America almost certainly would have collapsed long ago. Instead, its democracy has continued to grow and flower for most of the last two hundred years.

CHAPTER 4

DEMOCRACY FACES CHALLENGES

In the fall of 1863, America was being torn apart by the Civil War. The grand experiment in democracy had wreaked some ugly consequences. Northerners and Southerners could not agree on many things, and neither side could abide by the other's views any longer. The spirit of democracy is cooperation and compromise. But that spirit didn't apply to the issue of slavery. There was no middle ground. The train of democracy had derailed. Disagreement had turned into war.

SLAVERY IN AMERICA

Today, no American would consider a society in which slavery is legal as democratic. In fact, the United States equates democracy with freedom. However, for close to one hundred years after the United States was founded as a democracy, slavery was legal throughout the country, especially in the South. Few people, including abolitionists who called for an end to slavery, questioned whether the United States was a democracy. Nevertheless, many people, including Abraham Lincoln, argued that slavery was inconsistent with the principles behind democracy.

This rare photograph was taken at the Soldiers' National Cemetery in Gettysburg, Pennsylvania, where Lincoln gave his now-famous Gettysburg Address. Lincoln can be found facing the crowd, hatless, about an inch below the flag.

Abraham Lincoln's election as president in 1860 began a breakdown in American democracy. Proslavery Southern states refused to accept the antislavery Lincoln as president. Within months after Lincoln was inaugurated, eleven states seceded, or withdrew, from the Union. They formed the Confederate States of America. Lincoln was unprepared to see the nation fall apart. He clearly announced his intention to defend the Union with force if necessary. On April 12, 1861, Confederate forces launched a cannon attack on Fort Sumter in South Carolina. This action marked the start of the American Civil War, during which approximately 618,000 Americans died. Four years later, the Confederacy surrendered, and the nation became reunited.

The experience of the Civil War provides an important lesson in democracy. In order to survive, democracies need to have a civic culture in which the losers accept the results of free and fair elections. By so doing, they allow for the smooth transition between administrations and continuity in the democracy.

On January 1, 1863, during the Civil War, Lincoln issued the Emancipation Proclamation, freeing the slaves within the Confederate states. This marked the beginning of the end of the institution of slavery in the United States. Slavery was ended after the Civil War, but the war had not been a cure-all.

Lincoln had used war to force the South into submission and to free its slaves. But the entire plantation culture of the South was built on viewing blacks as less than human. Slaves were thought of as property, not people. It would take many years for that perception to change.

The Emancipation Proclamation was the first major step by the federal government to bring blacks within the folds of American democracy. See page 53 for a partial transcription.

THE GETTYSBURG ADDRESS

On November 19, a ceremony was held in Gettysburg, Pennsylvania. Four months earlier, Gettysburg had been the site of one of the Civil War's bloodiest battles. Thousands of men lost their lives there and part of the battlefield was being dedicated as a cemetery for the war dead. Fifteen thousand people attended the dedication.

President Abraham Lincoln's Gettysburg Address is widely thought to be one of the finest expressions of the meaning of democracy ever written. Lincoln began:

Four score and seven years ago, our fathers brought forth on this continent a new nation, conceived in liberty, and dedicated to the proposition that all men are created equal. Now, we are engaged in a great Civil War, testing whether that nation or any nation so conceived and so dedicated can long endure.

Lincoln didn't mean that the war was a test of whether democracy could work as a way to run a country. He meant the war was testing whether equality could ever really be the guiding principle of a nation. Lincoln continued:

It is for us, the living … to be dedicated here to the unfinished work which they who fought here have thus far so nobly advanced. It is … for us to be here dedicated to the great task remaining before us … that we here highly resolve that these dead shall not have died in vain; that this nation, under God, shall have a new birth of freedom, and that government of the people, by the people, for the people shall not perish from the Earth.

In the succinct, powerful phrase in Lincoln's last sentence —"of the people, by the people, for the people"—Lincoln created a vision of ideal democracy that has inspired and guided future generations.

BLACK CODES

After the Civil War, Congress was still controlled by the Northern states. It passed three Constitutional amendments to try to help blacks in America. The Thirteenth Amendment outlawed slavery. The Fourteenth guaranteed equal rights to all American citizens, regardless of their race. And the Fifteenth specifically guaranteed black men the right to vote.

The Southern states almost immediately started passing laws to undermine the new amendments. These were called black

This photograph, taken in May 1862, shows the slaves of the Confederate General Thomas F. Drayton of Hilton Head island, South Carolina.

This document is from the 1896 Supreme Court case *Plessy vs. Ferguson* that established the "separate but equal" provision legalizing segregation. *Brown vs. Board of Education* overturned it in 1954.

codes, and they restricted the rights of blacks. Some of them forced blacks to pass various tests before they'd be allowed to vote. Whites, of course, were exempt from the tests, not under the law, but in practice. Other black codes made sure that whites and blacks were kept separate in public life. Blacks had to go to separate schools, stay in separate hotels, eat in separate restaurants, and ride in separate cars on trains.

In 1896, the United States Supreme Court ruled in *Plessy vs. Ferguson* that it was constitutionally acceptable for states to require blacks and whites to use separate public facilities, as long as the facilities were roughly equal. The court's decision cleared the way for states—in both the North and the South—and the federal government to openly discriminate against African Americans. Segregation laws were rigidly enforced with both police measures and mob violence. As a result, African Americans were for decades relegated to the status of second-class citizens whose basic human rights were denied. Moreover, many states continued to set up obstacles to prevent blacks from voting.

Martin Luther King Jr. and his wife, Coretta Scott King (*center, right*) lead a march from Selma, Alabama, to Mongtomery, Alabama, to support voting rights for African Americans.

THE CIVIL RIGHTS MOVEMENT

Virtually all aspects of life for African Americans were subject to black codes. They affected where blacks could live, work, go to school, and even where they were born and died. Moreover, the facilities provided for blacks were markedly inferior to those reserved for whites. The doctrine of separate but equal established by the *Plessy vs. Ferguson* decision was in reality a myth.

The National Association for the Advancement of Colored people (NAACP) was formed in 1908 to fight segregation. After a series of legal challenges, the NAACP convinced the Supreme

Court in the 1954 case of *Brown vs. Board of Education* that segregational laws were unconstitutional. This court victory helped spur the civil rights movement of the late 1950s and 1960s. Led by Dr. Martin Luther King Jr., the movement successfully brought about a change in government policy and the public's attitude toward racial discrimination.

WOMEN AND THE VOTE

In most of the world's older democracies, women were denied the right to vote long after democracy was established as the system

A photograph, taken on May 4, 1912, shows a group of women suffragists lining up for a parade. The title of the photograph is *Youngest Parader in New York City Suffragist Parade.*

of government. In addition, women were also subject to other laws and customs that limited their rights to work, own property, publicly express their views, and enjoy an equal standing both at home and in public. By the mid-nineteenth century, women in the United States and other Western countries began demanding voting and other rights.

Led by Elizabeth Cady Stanton and Susan B. Anthony, among others, the women's suffrage movement in America agitated for voting rights throughout the second half of the nineteenth century and the early twentieth century. The movement's efforts began to pay off in 1869, when the Wyoming Territory extended equal suffrage to women. One by one, other states began allowing women to vote. However, the federal government did not grant women's suffrage until 1920. The first country to extend voting rights to women was New Zealand in 1893.

CHAPTER 5

CHARACTERISTICS OF DEMOCRACIES

A number of core principles make a nation democratic no matter where it is located in the world. Among these are the ideas of consent of the governed, as described by Jefferson in the Declaration of Independence, and a system of checks and balances among the executive, legislative, and judicial branches of governments. Other key features of democracies are free and fair elections, basic human rights, and the rule of law.

PROPER ELECTIONS

Elections are essential to representative democracy. However, the mere fact that a country holds elections does not make it a democracy. Many authoritarian governments hold elections to give the impression that they answer to the will of the people. However, these elections usually involve only candidates from a single party or only those of whom the government approve. Democratic elections must meet certain criteria. They should be competitive, periodic, inclusive, and definitive.

An election is considered to be competitive when it is open to opponents of the government. These opponents need to be free to speak and assemble in opposition to the government. Elections should be held at regular intervals. With the exception of judges, democratic elections should not place people in office for life. Voters are given periodic chances of selecting their leaders or representatives. Inclusive elections involve a large proportion of the adult population. An election that excludes a majority of the people cannot be said to be democratic. Consequently, during the era of apartheid when more than 80 percent of the population was denied the vote, South Africa was not a democracy. Elections are definitive when they determine the leaders of government, not just symbolic offices.

Voting in democratic elections is usually done by private ballots. In other words, voters cast their votes in secret. This minimizes the risk of voters being intimidated into voting for a particular candidate or issue. However, the counting of the votes and the management of the elections must be conducted as openly as possible to assure the citizens that the results are accurate.

A common electoral feature in all democracies is that citizens are grouped into constituencies, or zones, such as a congressional district in the United States or a parliamentary constituency in the United Kingdom. However, most democracies have particular features or a combination of features that distinguishes them from the others. Nevertheless, there are two main types of electoral systems in the world: plurality elections and proportional elections. The plurality electoral system is often described as "winner takes all" because only the candidate who gets the most votes in the constituency is elected. This system is used in US presidential, congressional, gubernatorial, and most local government elections. Under this system, a person can be elected to office with less than 50 percent of the votes. In some instances, where the election is between two or more candidates and none receives 50 percent of the votes, a second run-off election is held between the candidates with the two highest vote tallies.

President-elect Donald Trump, a Republican, gives his acceptance speech after defeating Democratic rival Hillary Clinton in late 2016. Trump's family and close associates join him onstage at the New York Hilton Midtown, a hotel in Manhattan.

In proportional elections, more than one candidate is elected to represent each constituency. The results are based on the proportion of the votes that a party or a candidate receives. A major advantage of this system is that minority groups, parties, and views have a better chance of being represented in the lawmaking bodies. Proportional representation is used in South Africa and in many western European democracies, including Germany, Finland, and Austria.

SHOULD THE UNITED STATES KEEP THE ELECTORAL COLLEGE?

During the 2016 US presidential election, Republican contender Donald Trump triumphed by receiving 304 electoral votes to Democratic rival Hillary Clinton's 227. However, Clinton received about 2.9 million more popular votes than Trump, according to the Pew Research Center. The tally indicates that Clinton won with 65.8 million votes to almost 63 million for Trump.

Usually, presidents who win their elections do so with more popular votes than their opponent. Five times in US history that expectation has been disrupted, including the 2016 election. The upset victory by Trump renewed a longstanding debate: should the US maintain the Electoral College system of choosing the president? ProCon.org, a nonprofit, nonpartisan charity designed to explore such issues, came up with a list of pros and cons to help answer that question.

Pros include: a guarantee of safeguarding against uninformed and uneducated voters by allowing an elector to carry out the will of the majority in their area; the Electoral College ensures that all parts of the country are involved in the presidential elections, not just those highly-populated areas; and the electoral method guarantees certainty about the election results without the need for multiple recounts.

Cons against the system involve: more public access to information than at the time the Constitution was written, allowing for a more educated electorate; it gives too much power to a handful of swing states that are not firmly in the grips of one political party or another; and it ignores the will of the people since there are just 538 electors versus more than 350 million Americans.

HUMAN RIGHTS

The idea of everyone possessing certain basic rights is a cornerstone to modern democracies. Jefferson described these rights in the Declaration of Independence as being "unalienable." He meant that all human beings are entitled to these rights. Most democracies have their own list of basic human rights. However, the inalienable rights have been widely accepted to be freedom of speech, freedom of religion, freedom of assembly, and the right to equal protection under the law.

A rebel stronghold near Damascus, Syria, suffers an attack by government forces. Syria's dictator President Bashar al-Assad has long been accused of human rights violations by the United States.

Freedom of speech is the right to express one's opinions or ideas without fear of government reprisals. When citizens fear voicing their opinions, governments are less responsive—and less accountable—to them. Freedom of the press is an important aspect of free speech. An independent press—one that is not controlled by the government—is essential to the spread of ideas. The press in a democracy informs the public about what the government and others are doing. By doing so, the press empowers citizens to make informed decisions.

Freedom of assembly is closely tied to freedom of speech. Citizens must be free to meet to discuss and debate ideas. Freedom of assembly allows citizens the right to form or join organizations such as political parties and interest groups. It also gives them the right to lead organized protests. This way, individual citizens can demonstrate the strength of their positions and can more effectively challenge the government.

The idea that no one should be required to practice a particular religion against his or her choosing is known as freedom of religion. It also means that no one should be punished for his or her religious beliefs or not practicing any religion at all. The United States follows a long-standing policy of separation of church and state. Accordingly, it has no national religion. Many other democratic countries, including Italy and Spain, have officially established or endorsed churches or religions. Nevertheless, their governments are required to protect religious minorities.

Equal protection under the law really means freedom from discrimination. In other words, the laws of a democratic nation should apply evenly and equally to, among others, rich and poor, ethnic and religious minorities, and opponents of the government. Equal protection under the law is also related to another major tenet of democratic societies: the rule of law.

EQUAL PROTECTION AND DUE PROCESS

The two main components of the rule of law are the notions of equal protection and due process. Equal protection dictates that no one should be above the law (receive special privileges) or below the law (subject to discrimination). The principle of due process of law holds that the rules and procedures that a democratic government follows in enforcing the laws should be clearly and publicly known and should not be exercised arbitrarily. Over time, a number of guarantees have been adopted as standards in democratic countries. They include:

- Police should not break into and search a home without a court order showing good reason for the search.
- No one should be arrested without explicit written charges specifying the suspected violation.
- A person under arrest should be freed immediately if the court finds that the charge is unwarranted or the arrest is invalid. This doctrine is known as habeas corpus.
- No one can be compelled to be a witness against himself or herself.
- No one should be subject to cruel and unusual punishment, according to the laws and customs of the society.
- A person under arrest is entitled to a speedy trial.
- No one should be tried for the same crime twice. Therefore, a person who is acquitted of a crime can never be charged with that crime again.

Some of these guarantees date back as far as the Magna Carta of 1215. In the United States, many are embedded in the Bill of Rights and other constitutional amendments.

The citizens depend on an independent judiciary to make sure that the executive and legislative branches of government do not compromise them.

CURRENT CONCERNS IN DEMOCRACY

In the United States, as well as in other democracies, the meaning and scope of democracy continue to be debated. The issue of gay, lesbian, bisexual, and transgender rights is a new frontier in basic human rights. Although these individuals are not denied suffrage, advocacy groups continue to push for the acceptance of same sex marriage around the world.

Electronic voting poses new concerns about fraud, especially in regards to the efforts of hostile governments against democracies like the attempted Russian interference with the 2016 presidential election in the United States.

According to Freedom House, a nonprofit organization that monitors freedom and democracies around the world, there are eighty-seven free countries in the world, and fifty-nine partly free countries as of 2017. There are more democracies in the world than other political systems. Although that number has remained steady for some time, some countries have joined the ranks of democracies while others have fallen from it. Democracy is not guaranteed. It requires the active participation of citizens to make sure that those who govern do so with their consent.

640 BCE   The world's first known democratic government is established in the Greek city-state of Sparta.

508 BCE   Democracy begins in Athens.

404 BCE   Sparta conquers Athens and puts an end to Athenian democracy.

1215 CE   England's King John is forced to sign the Magna Carta.

1450   The Mohawk, Onandaga, Seneca, Oneida, and Cayuga Native Americans join together under the Great Binding Law to create the Iroquois Confederation.

1762   The French philosopher Jean-Jacques Rosseau publishes *The Social Contract*, in which he further advances the cause of democracy.

1775   The American Revolution begins.

1776   The Continental Congress formally adopts Thomas Jefferson's Declaration of Independence.

1787   The US Constitution is drafted.

1861–1865   The American Civil War is waged.

1863   President Abraham Lincoln issues the Emancipation Proclamation.

1893   New Zealand becomes the first country to grant women's suffrage.

1920   The Nineteenth Amendment is passed, guaranteeing women the right to vote in the United States.

2016   Donald Trump wins the election for US president despite losing the popular vote.

THE MAGNA CARTA

Transcription Excerpt

(1) FIRST, THAT WE HAVE GRANTED TO GOD, and by this present charter have confirmed for us and our heirs in perpetuity, that the English Church shall be free, and shall have its rights undiminished, and its liberties unimpaired. That we wish this so to be observed, appears from the fact that of our own free will, before the outbreak of the present dispute between us and our barons, we granted and confirmed by charter the freedom of the Church's elections—a right reckoned to be of the greatest necessity and importance to it—and caused this to be confirmed by Pope Innocent III. This freedom we shall observe ourselves, and desire to be observed in good faith by our heirs in perpetuity. (12) No 'scutage' or 'aid' may be levied in our kingdom without its general consent, unless it is for the ransom of our person, to make our eldest son a knight, and (once) to marry our eldest daughter. For these purposes only a reasonable 'aid' may be levied. 'Aids' from the city of London are to be treated similarly. (39) No free man shall be seized or imprisoned, or stripped of his rights or possessions, or outlawed or exiled, or deprived of his standing in any other way, nor will we proceed with force against him, or send others to do so, except by the lawful judgement of his equals or by the law of the land.

DECLARATION OF INDEPENDENCE

Transcription Excerpt

We hold these truths to be self-evident, that all men are created equal, that they are endowed by their Creator with certain unalienable Rights, that among these are Life, Liberty and the pursuit of Happiness.— That to secure these rights, Governments are instituted among Men, deriving their just powers from the consent of the governed, —That whenever any Form of Government becomes destructive of these ends, it is the Right of the People to alter or to abolish it, and to institute new Government, laying its foundation on such principles and organizing its powers in such form, as to them shall seem most likely to effect their Safety and Happiness. Prudence, indeed, will dictate that Governments long established should not be changed for light and transient causes; and accordingly all experience hath shewn, that mankind are more disposed to suffer, while evils are sufferable, than to right themselves by abolishing the forms to which they are accustomed. But when a long train of abuses and usurpations, pursuing invariably the same Object evinces a design to reduce them under absolute Despotism, it is their right, it is their duty, to throw off such Government, and to provide new Guards for their future security.

ARTICLES OF CONFEDERATION

Transcription Excerpt

Article I. The Stile of this confederacy shall be "The United States of America."

Article II. Each state retains its sovereignty, freedom, and independence, and every Power, Jurisdiction and right, which is not by this confederation expressly delegated to the United States, in Congress assembled.

Article III. The said states hereby severally enter into a firm league of friendship with each other, for their common defense, the security of their Liberties, and their mutual and general welfare, binding themselves to assist each other, against all force offered to, or attacks made upon them, or any of them, on account of religion, sovereignty, trade, or any other pretence whatever.

UNITED STATES CONSTITUTION

Transcription Excerpt

We the People of the United States, in Order to form a more perfect Union, establish Justice, insure domestic Tranquility, provide for the common defence, promote the general Welfare, and secure the Blessings of Liberty to ourselves and our Posterity, do ordain and establish this Constitution for the United States of America.

Article. I.
Section. 1.
All legislative Powers herein granted shall be vested in a Congress of the United States, which shall consist of a Senate and House of Representatives.

Article. II.
Section. 1.
The executive Power shall be vested in a President of the United States of America. He shall hold his Office during the Term of four Years, and, together with the Vice President, chosen for the same Term, be elected, as follows.

Article III.
Section. 1.
The judicial Power of the United States, shall be vested in one supreme Court, and in such inferior Courts as the Congress may from time to time ordain and establish. The Judges, both of the supreme and inferior Courts, shall hold their Offices during good Behaviour, and shall, at stated Times, receive for their Services, a Compensation, which shall not be diminished during their Continuance in Office.

EMANCIPATION PROCLAMATION

Transcription Excerpt

By the President of the United States of America:

A Proclamation.

Whereas, on the twenty-second day of September, in the year of our Lord one thousand eight hundred and sixty-two, a proclamation was issued by the President of the United States, containing, among other things, the following, to wit:

That on the first day of January, in the year of our Lord one thousand eight hundred and sixty-three, all persons held as slaves within any State or designated part of a State, the people whereof shall then be in rebellion against the United States, shall be then, thenceforward, and forever free; and the Executive Government of the United States, including the military and naval authority thereof, will recognize and maintain the freedom of such persons, and will do no act or acts to repress such persons, or any of them, in any efforts they may make for their actual freedom.

GLOSSARY

AMENDMENT An addition made to a document at a later date.

AUTOCRACY A government in which one person or small group of persons hold unlimited power.

BLASPHEMY The act of attacking official or traditional beliefs.

BODY A governmental institution, such as the legislature or a court.

CITY-STATE A city and the villages that surround it. Roughly comparable to a county, except it had its own completely independent government.

CONSTITUTION The document that defines the fundamental rules of a government.

DELEGATE A person selected or appointed to represent a group of people in a governmental body.

ELECTORAL COLLEGE A group of people representing the states of the US, who cast formal votes for the election of the president and vice president.

FEDERAL Having to do with a whole country, as opposed to its individual states or territories.

LEGISLATION A document that establishes a law.

MAGNA CARTA The agreement made in 1215 between King John of England and his barons, which for the first time gave them some rights that even the king could not violate. It was the first step away from monarchy and toward democracy in Europe.

MILITARISTIC Fixated on military might or given to starting wars.

MONARCHY A system in which a king or queen holds absolute power over a nation.

OPPRESS To use power to mistreat or keep down a person or members of a group.

PHILOSOPHER Someone who uses reason to analyze the way the world is and the way it should be.

REPRESENTATIVE DEMOCRACY A system in which people elect delegates to speak for their interests in the government.

SCORE A period of twenty years.

SELF-EVIDENT Obvious.

SOLIDARITY An act of unity with an oppressed person or group of people.

SUSTAINABLE Able to be maintained indefinitely.

TERM LIMITS A restriction on how a long a person is allowed to hold an office in his or her government. For example, no one can be US president for more than eight consecutive years.

TYRANT A ruler who uses absolute power unjustly to oppress his subjects.

UNALIENABLE Something that cannot be taken away.

American Independence Museum
One Governors Lane
Exeter, NH 03833
(603) 772-2622
Website: https://www.independencemuseum.org
Facebook: @americanindependencemuseum
The museum educates, studies, and celebrates the people, places, and events that led to the founding of the United States.

Canadian Museum of History
100 Laurier Street
Gatineau, QC K1A 0M8
Canada
(800) 555-5621
Website: http://www.historymuseum.ca
Facebook/Twitter/Instagram: @CanMusHistory
The museum features exhibits on the founding of Canada as well as its political challenges.

Democracy Watch
PO Box 821, Stn. B
Ottawa, ON K1P 5P9
Canada
(613) 241-5179
Email: info@democracywatch.ca
Website: https://democracywatch.ca
Facebook: @DemocracyWatch
Twitter: @DemocracyWatchr

As a nonprofit, nonpartisan organization, the citizen group advocates democratic reform, accountability of the government and corporate responsibility.

Independence National Historical Park
143 S. 3rd Street
Philadelphia, PA 19106
(215) 965-2305
Website: https://www.nps.gov/inde/index.htm
Facebook and Twitter: @indepdenceNHP
Instagram: @independencenps
The park includes a number of locations: the Liberty Bell Center, Independence Hall, Congress Hall, the Second Bank of the United States, Washington Square, and more. The visitor center provides park rangers that lead walking tours.

Library of Congress
101 Independence Ave, SE
Washington, DC 20540
(202) 707-5000
Website: http://www.loc.gov
Facebook: @libraryofcongress
Twitter and Instagram: @librarycongress
Multiple collections reveal American history in art, documents, and artifacts from the exploration to the political foundation of the Americas.

Martin Luther King, Jr., Papers Project at Stanford University
Cypress Hall, D Wing
466 Via Ortega
Stanford, CA 94305-4146
(650) 723-2092
Email: kinginstitute@stanford.edu

Website: http://www.stanford.edu/group/King
Facebook: @KingInstitute
Twitter: @mlk_institute
The project houses the most complete collection of King's most important unpublished manuscripts, letters, sermons, speeches, and published pieces.

National Democratic Institute
455 Massachusetts Avenue NW, 8th Floor
Washington, DC 20001-2621
(202) 728-5500
Website: https://www.ndi.org
Facebook: @National.Democratic.Institute
Twitter: @NDI
Instagram: @ndidemocracy
The National Democratic Institute is a nonprofit, nonpartisan, nongovernmental organization that has supported democratic institutions and practices in every region of the world for more than three decades.

US National Archives and Records Administration
700 Pennsylvania Avenue NW
Washington, DC 20408
86-NARA-NARA (toll free)
Website: http://www.archives.gov/welcome/index.html
Facebook: @usnationalarchives
Twitter and Instagram: @usnatarchives
The archives facilitates democracy by providing public access to important government records. The records allow citizens to hold their government accountable to their actions.

FOR FURTHER READING

Collier, Elise. *Constitutional Democracy.* New York, NY: Rosen Publishing, 2018.

Connolly, Sean. *Democracy*. London, UK: Franklin Watts, 2017.

Duignan, Brian. *Forms of Government and the Rise of Democracy*. New York, NY: Rosen Publishing, 2013.

Lowery, Zoe. *The American Revolution.* New York, NY: Rosen Publishing, 2016.

Lowery, Zoe. *Democracy.* New York, NY: Britannica Educational Publishing, 2015.

Machajewski, Sarah. *Declaration of Independence.* New York, NY: Rosen Publishing, 2017.

Maloof, Torrey. *George Washington and the Men Who Shaped America*. Huntington Beach, CA: Teacher Created Materials, 2016.

Nelson, Kristen Rajczak. *U.S. Constitution*. New York, NY: Rosen Publishing, 2017.

Perkins, Anne. *Trailblazers in Politics.* New York, NY: Rosen Publishing, 2015.

Witmer, Scott. *Political Systems.* Oxford, UK: Capstone Global Library Ltd., 2013.

BIBLIOGRAPHY

Arthur, John. *Democracy: Theory and Practice*. Belmont, CA: Wadsworth Publishing Company, 1992.

Church, Forrest. *The American Creed: A Spiritual and Patriotic Primer*. New York, NY: St. Martin's Press, 2002.

DeSilver, Drew. "Trump's Victory Another Example of How Electoral College Wins Are Bigger than Popular Vote Ones." Pew Research Center, December 20, 2016. http://www.pewresearch.org/fact-tank/2016/12/20/why-electoral-college-landslides-are-easier-to-win-than-popular-vote-ones.

Freedom House. "Populists and Autocrats: The Dual Threat to Global Democracy." Retrieved on May 5, 2018. https://freedomhouse.org/report/freedom-world/freedom-world-2017.

King, Martin Luther Jr. *The Autobiography of Martin Luther King, Jr.* New York, NY: Warner Books, 2001.

O'Neil, James. *The Origins and Development of Ancient Greek Democracy*. Lanham, MD: Rowman & Littlefield Publishing, 2002.

Parker, A. C. *The Constitution of the Five Nations, or the Iroquois Book of the Great Law*. Oshweken, ON: Iroqrafts, 1991.

PBS. "The Populace of Athens—Slaves." Retrieved on May 5, 2018. http://www.pbs.org/empires/thegreeks/background/32b.html.

Pearson, Ellen Holmes. "Iroquois and the Founding Fathers." George Mason University. Retrieved on May 5, 2018. http://teachinghistory.org/history-content/ask-a-historian/24099.

ProCon.org. "The Electoral College Top 3 Pros and Cons." September 1, 2017. https://www.procon.org/headline.php?headlineID=005330.

Roser, Max. "Democracy." University of Oxford. Retrieved on May 5, 2018. https://ourworldindata.org/democracy.

Simon, James. *What Kind of Nation: Thomas Jefferson, John Marshall and the Epic Struggle to Create a United States*. New York, NY: Simon & Schuster, 2002.

Wills, Garry. *Inventing America: Jefferson's Declaration of Independence*. Boston, MA: Mariner Books, 2002.

Wills, Garry. *Lincoln at Gettysburg: The Words that Remade America*. New York, NY: Touchstone Books, 1993.

INDEX

ABOUT THE AUTHORS

Xina M. Uhl discovered her love of history while still in grade school. She went on to obtain a master of arts in history from California State University, Northridge. After teaching college-level American history, she moved into educational writing. She has authored books, textbooks, teachers' guides, lessons, and assessment questions in the field of history. When she is not writing or reading she enjoys travel, photography, and hiking with her dogs. Her blog features her travel adventures and latest fiction projects.

Bill Stites is a writer from New York City.

PHOTO CREDITS

Cover (Statue of Liberty) Luciano Mortula - LGM/Shutterstock.com; cover (Constitution) Stephen Coburn/Shutterstock.com; cover (George Washington) John Parrot/Stocktrek Images /Getty Images; p. 5 Private Collection/Bridgeman Images; p. 7 Print Collector/Hulton Archive/Getty Images; p. 9 Hercules Milas /Alamy Stock Photo; p. 11 DEA/G. Dagli Orti/DeAgostini /Getty Images; pp. 14, 25, 30, 37 National Archives; p. 16 Library of Congress, Manuscript Division; pp. 19, 33, 34, 36, 39 Library of Congress, Prints and Photographs Division; p. 20 Burstein Collection/Corbis Historical/Getty Images; p. 23 GraphicaArtis /Archive Photos/Getty Images; p. 27 National Park Service; p. 38 William Lovelace/Hulton Archive/Getty Images; p. 43 Spencer Platt/Getty Images; p. 45 Abdulmonam Eassa/AFP/Getty Images; chapter opener pages (world map silhouette) Vectorios2016 /DigitalVision Vectors/Getty Images.

Design and Layout: Nicole Russo-Duca; Photo Researcher: Nicole DiMella